RUTH

A Woman Whose Loyalty Was Stronger Than Her Grief

By Marlee Alex

Illustrated by Alfonso Ruano

SCANDINAVIA

Ruth

A Woman Whose Loyalty Was Stronger than Her Grief
Written by Marlee Alex
Illustrated by Alfonso Ruano
Graphic design by Nils V. Glistrup
Copyright © Scandinavia Publishing House
Drejervej 11-21, DK-2400 Copenhagen NV, Denmark
Telephone: (+45) 35 31 03 32
Fax: (+45) 35 31 03 34
E-mail: jvo@scanpublishing.dk
Homepage: www.scanpublishg.dk
Text Copyright © 1994 Marlee Alex
Conceived, designed and produced by
Scandinavia Publishing House
Drejervej 11-21, DK-2400 Copenhagen NV, Denmark
Holy unto the LORD
ISBN NO.: 87 7247 5412
Printed in Singapore

RUTH

A Woman Whose Loyalty
Was Stronger Than Her Grief

By Marlee Alex

Illustrated by Alfonso Ruano

SCANDINAVIA

Once upon a time there was a young woman named Ruth who lived in the land of Moab. Ruth was married to a nice young man whose mother, Naomi, lived with them. Ruth and Naomi were good friends. Nearby lived Naomi's oldest son and his wife, Orpha. They were all one close family.

For several years life was good. Ruth had no children of her own, but she was content and happy. Yet not in her wildest dreams did she imagine she would one day be the great-grandmother of a mighty king.

ears passed. Then the husbands of both Ruth and Orpha died. It was a very sad time. Ruth and Orpha missed their husbands terribly, and Naomi missed her two sons. Besides grieving for their loved ones, the women were worried about the future. In those days, a woman could not take a job and earn a living for herself. Now there was no one to take care of Ruth and Orpha and their mother-in-law, Naomi.

Naomi sat down with the two younger women. Tears filled her eyes. "Ten years ago I came from the land of Israel," she said. "I was born, raised and married there. My two sons were born there before we moved to Moab. Now that they are dead I feel homesick for my own country. So I've decided to go back to Israel where people worship the one true God. Besides, the crops have been good there this year. There will be plenty to eat. I'll get along all right."

Ruth interrupted, "But, dear Naomi, what shall we do? We love you as if you were our own mother."

Naomi answered, "You are welcome to come with me if you like. But it would be better for you to return to the homes of your parents here in Moab. They could help each of you find another husband. You should get married again, and raise families of your own. You deserve better lives than I could ever provide you."

Naomi kissed Ruth and held her tight, then she turned to Orpha and hugged her. "I love both of you as if you were my own children. You have truly been loyal daughters to me," she said tenderly. "Go on home now, for I have nothing left to give you."

Ruth was crying. Then Orpha started crying. Naomi stopped trying to fight back her own tears. The women thought they would never see each other again. Orpha kissed Naomi once more, then packed her things and returned to the home of her childhood.

But Ruth clung to Naomi and cried, "I want to go with you to Israel. I want to stay with you."

Naomi insisted, "Look Ruth, Orpha has gone back to her own people. You must do the same."

"Please don't make me go back!" Ruth pleaded. "I want to go wherever you go, and live wherever you live. I want to become one of the people of Israel, like you, and worship the one true God. When I die, I want to be buried beside you."

Ruth was not going to change her mind. So Naomi did not say another word.

The two women set off for Israel on foot. After many days and nights they finally arrived in Bethlehem, the village where Naomi had grown up. Ruth and Naomi were tired. They had no more money. They were hungry and thirsty. Their feet were blistered and sore.

Everyone in Bethlehem was very busy, for the barley harvest had just begun. But people stopped and stared, wondering who the two strangers were. Then an elderly lady recognized her old friend. "Could this possibly be Naomi?" she asked.

"You must not call me Naomi anymore," Naomi answered, "for that name means

'pleasant'. My life is not pleasant anymore. Call me a name that means 'bitter' now, for that is how I feel. I left this town full and happy, but I am returning empty." Naomi was feeling sorry for herself. But Ruth determined to cheer her up.

After a good night's sleep, Ruth said to Naomi, "I'll try to get something for us to eat. The barley is being harvested now. Perhaps I can gather some of the grain left over in the fields. Then we can make barley soup."

So Ruth tied a scarf on her head and left for the countryside. She asked permission to gather the leftover grain at the first field she came to, then began to work along the edges of the field. The field belonged to a man named Boaz. Ruth did not know Boaz was a relative of Naomi.

That afternoon Boaz came out to the field to inspect the harvest. "Who is that girl over there?" he asked his workers.

"She's new in town," one of them answered. "She is Naomi's daughter-in-law, from Moab. She was out here bright and early this morning and has hardly stopped to rest."

Boaz called to Ruth. "Hello!" he shouted. "It's quite all right. You can stay in my field and take whatever grain has fallen behind the reapers. Just keep behind the women.

I'll make sure none of the men bother you. And when you get thirsty, drink from the water jars my servants fill."

Ruth was amazed that Boaz was so friendly. "Why are you being so kind to a stranger like me?" she asked.

'Well, I know who you are!" Boaz replied. You are Naomi's daughter-in-law. I've heard about how good you have been to her. You even left your own mother and father in Moab to come to Israel and make a home under the wings of the Lord God. May God bless you and your work!"

"Oh, thank you sir!" Ruth exclaimed. "And thank you for your kindness even though I haven't been hired by you."

At lunch time Boaz called out, "Come, Ruth. You can share our food." Ruth joined Boaz and the other reapers. She was given all the roasted grain and bread she could eat. She wrapped some of it in her scarf to take home to Naomi.

14

When Ruth returned to the field after lunch, Boaz told his servants, "Let her take all the grain she wants. In fact, I want you to pull up some stalks of grain and drop them on purpose for her to find."

Ruth continued working until evening, then returned to Naomi. Ruth beat the grain from the straw, and discovered there was enough barley to fill a large basket. That much barley would last a long time.

Naomi was surprised and pleased. "Where in the world did you get all this, Ruth? Someone must have been very kind to you. Bless his heart! Tell me, how did you manage to gather so much?"

Ruth told Naomi all about Boaz and what had happened that day.

"Praise the Lord!" Naomi exclaimed. "Did you know this man, Boaz, is a relative of ours?"

"No, but I wondered why he was so kind to me. He even told me I could stay and gather grain in his field until the end of harvest!"

"That's wonderful Ruth. And if you keep close to the other women reapers like Boaz said, you'll be safe. I won't have to worry about you at all."

R uth and Naomi had plenty to eat all summer long, and began to build a new life. Then one day Naomi said to Ruth, "It is time you were getting married again, Ruth. I'd like to help you find a good man."

"Naomi, we are doing just fine. God will continue to provide for us," Ruth responded.

But Naomi acted as if she hadn't heard Ruth. "What about Boaz?" Naomi continued. "After all, he has been kind. He would be a good husband. You know, he'll be working this evening out on the threshing floor."

"But Naomi," Ruth answered, "to be kind is one thing. To take a wife is quite another thing. Are you sure this is the right way to go about getting a husband?"

Naomi explained, "In this country, when a man dies, it is the custom for his closest relative to take care of his family. Boaz is our relative. It would be natural and right for him to marry you."

Ruth finally agreed, "All right, Naomi, I'll do whatever you say."

"Listen, my daughter. Here's what you do. Take a warm bath and put on your nicest dress. Dab a little perfume behind your ears, too. Then go down to the threshing floor where Boaz is working, but don't let him see you. When he has finished his evening meal and lies down, you wait until he has fallen asleep. Then go and curl up at his feet."

That night, Boaz woke up and noticed someone lying at his feet. "Who are you?" he whispered in the darkness.

"I am Ruth, your close relative." Ruth replied. "I am here to seek your protection. I need the security of a good marriage."

"Why, Ruth! May the Lord bless you," exclaimed Boaz. "Your loyalty to me is as great as your loyalty to Naomi. You are willing to marry me, instead of seeking a younger man? Everyone in Bethlehem knows you are an outstanding woman. To take you as my wife would be an honor."

So Boaz and Ruth were married. And months later, a son was born to them.

Naomi was happy to become a grandmother. She exclaimed, "Ruth, you have been a greater blessing to me than seven sons. This little grandchild makes me feel young again!"

Naomi's neighbors said, "We think you should name this boy 'Obed'. Perhaps he will be famous someday!" (And Obed did become the grandfather of Israel's greatest king, King David.)

R uth had been loyal toward Naomi in spite of her own sadness and grief. She had followed Naomi to Israel and worked hard to start a new life for both of them. Then Boaz showed kindness to Ruth.

He took care of her and loved her. Ruth became a mother. She will be remembered as the great-grandmother of a good and mighty king, and as a woman who was a true friend.

You can find the story of Ruth in the Old Testament
in the book of Ruth.